HERE'S TO YOUR HEALTH

"Things you need to know about the health benefits, uses, and properties of Cinnamon."

Kimyatta Grimes

CHAPTER ONE

Cinnamon - The Spice of Life

Cinnamon originates from the bark of Evergreen trees of the family Cinnamomum. When cinnamon is gathered, the bark is peeled and dried. As it dries, cinnamon twists into an understood shape, called plumes. It is then sold as entire cinnamon or cinnamon sticks. Cinnamon is accessible in either sticks or as ground powder. There are two cinnamon varieties.

1. Ceylon cinnamon: Also known as "True" cinnamon starts particularly from the tree known as Cinnamomum Zeylanicum. Ceylon cinnamon has a flavor that is sweeter and more unique than the cassia variety. It is normally more costly and harder to discover than the cassia cinnamon as it is native to Sri Lanka.

Ceylon cinnamon is associated with the lives of people in Sri Lanka, emotionally, socially and economically. For them it is the spice of life. Ceylon cinnamon groves are located in the Western and South-Western regions of the island.

The tropical sunshine and abundant rain in these areas provide the ideal habitat for the growth of cinnamon. The sweetest, most prized variety grows in the 'Silver Sand' coastal belt of Sri Lanka.

2. Cassia Cinnamon: This is the more basic assortment today, what individuals by and large allude to as "cinnamon." For this reason cassia is utilized all the more fre□uently as a part of American kitchens than Ceylon cinnamon.

Cinnamon is recognized as a helper for respiratory, digestive, and gynecological diseases. Later studies rising up out of western nations have demonstrated numerous possible advantageous wellbeing impacts of cinnamon, for example, calming properties, hostile to microbial action and blood glucose control, decreasing cardiovascular infection, boosting subjective capacity, and diminishing the danger of colonic tumor.

Cinnamon has a high level of Manganese which is utilized to strengthen bones, blood and other connective tissues, as indicated by the University of Maryland Medical Center. The body needs manganese for ideal bone wellbeing, so individuals who are lacking in the mineral can probably develop osteoporosis. Obviously another component bringing about Osteoporosis might be extreme dairy utilization.

Immaculate Cinnamon Leaf oil smells incredible as well. It is a powerful scent neutralizer as it eliminates a microorganism that makes awful smells and not simply to veil smells. You can use 2-5 drops of Cinnamon leaf oil blended with water on a diffuser and inside of minutes scents are killed. On the other hand, spray weakened Cinnamon Leaf Oil and wipe down toilets, floors and kitchen ledges, trash bins and the inside of vehicles to <uickly eradicate foul smells.

 It smells fresher than most compound sprays. It likewise has the impact of enhancing your state of mind.

Cinnamon is a well-known warming specialist. It can be mixed with carrier oil, it is highly effective in relaxing and relieving muscle pain. You can add a few drops into your bath to relax and to soothe tired and aching muscles. Also cinnamon oil is ideal for massaging as well as an ointment for arthritis.

Also cinnamon has remarkable cleansing extracts which are very useful for the cleansing process. A facial pack made with cinnamon powder (make sure it is Ceylon cinnamon) and bee honey can result in removing blackheads, whiteheads and cleaning your face the same as many expensive artificial packs.

The catechin antioxidants contained in cinnamon may help in the reduction of oral cancers. Polyphenols and tannin act as antibiotics, thus inhibiting bacteria that can cause tooth decay. Cinnamon contains fluoride, which fights bad breath and prevents tooth decay by eradicating harmful bacteria from the oral cavity. A daily dose of two cups made from cinnamon provides around 1.5 mg fluoride.

Use of cinnamon

Cinnamon is principally used as a condiment and added flavoring in cooking. Its flavor is due to an essential oil that makes up 0.5% to 1% of its composition. This oil has a golden-yellow color, an easily recognizable odor and a very hot aromatic taste.

In the Middle East, Persia and Turkey, cinnamon powder is added to a wide variety of sweet and savory dishes. In the USA, a cinnamon-sugar mix is used to flavor cereals, bread-based dishes (eg, cinnamon toast), and fruits (eg, cinnamon apple).

Cinnamon is also used in the making of chocolate and many desserts, such as apple pie, doughnuts, cinnamon buns, spicy candies, coffee, tea, hot cocoa and liqueurs.

Nutritional value of cinnamon

- Ten grams (about 2.1 teaspoons) of ground cinnamon contain:
- Fat: 0.12 grams (1.2%)
- Carbohydrates: 8.06g (80%) of which fibers: 5.31g (53.1%) and sugars: 0.2g (2%)
- Protein: 0.4g (4%)

How Cinnamon Regulates Your Glucose Level

We've always known cinnamon as the ingredient that makes cinnamon rolls so irresistibly yummy. It is commonly used as an ingredient for the best cinnamon rolls, apple cinnamon pie, pastries and as flavoring for tea, coffee and various types of baked desserts, and as scent for candles, incense and essential oils.

Aside from its culinary wonder, there are many more benefits of cinnamon powder. It can be used as medicine to treat a variety of ailments. It has been highlighted as a spice that can lower blood sugar or glucose level as manifested in Type 2 diabetic patients.

This was the result of a study conducted among 60 subjects where patients who have been suffering from this particular illness were given small doses of cinnamon. The results were amazing. Cinnamon did not only lower the patients' glucose level but also significantly lowered their cholesterol level coupled with an increase in the body's natural production of insulin.

Cinnamon's action is to slow down the rate of digestion of food in the stomach, consequently reducing the production of glucose or blood sugar in the body. Therefore adding small amounts of cinnamon powder in your diet can significantly bring down your blood sugar level providing you some relief from your present ordeal.

Interestingly, it can stimulate brain activity merely by sniffing its strong aroma. This is a better alternative to those who dislike its strong flavor and taste. Just by constantly smelling the spice can improve your intellectual ability and develop your thinking and reasoning skills as well as improve your memory.

CHAPTER TWO

How to Use and Store Cinnamon

True cinnamon is a spice that comes from the bark of a tropical tree related to the bay laurel. It can be bought ground into a fine powder or as ⬜uills which are pieces of the bark curled into a cylindrical shape. A cheaper version of cinnamon which is very similar in taste to the real thing comes from the bark of the cassia tree. This also comes ground or in ⬜uills.

If you are only concerned with the taste, then the cheaper version is fine. However, cinnamon is also good for you. Research has shown it can help reduce cholesterol and help to stabilise blood sugar. Like many spices, it is also high in antioxidants. For this reason, many prefer to use the true cinnamon.

To keep your cinnamon fresher longer, buy the ⬜uills and grind them in a spice grinder as needed. Ground spices will start to lose their flavor within a month. Exposure to light, moisture and air will also deplete the flavor very □uickly. To keep your cinnamon fresh, store it in an airtight container, in a dry, cool place away from direct light.

You can boost the flavour of cinnamon by toasting it briefly in a dry skillet or fry pan. Only a few minutes is necessary, until the spice turns slightly brown and aromatic.

There are many ways to use cinnamon to add delicious flavor to your food. Try a sprinkle of cinnamon on your morning coffee, toast or oatmeal. Add cinnamon to your cakes or cookies. Enhance the flavour of chilli or curry by adding a teaspoon of cinnamon. Baked sweet potatoes are delicious with a sprinkle of cinnamon. Custard or cheesecake take on a new flavor with a dusting of cinnamon. Give a new twist to yogurt by stirring cooked apple and cinnamon through it.

Health Benefits of Cinnamon

Cinnamon is considered one of the oldest spices and unsurpassed ingredient in the kitchen. It has a very pleasant smell and taste and is used as an addition to fruit salads, pies, and other desserts. Many people like coffee that is sprinkled with a little cinnamon, because it gets a special flavor. It may also be added to tea and other drinks.

In fact, one has to distinguish between two types of cinnamon. One is Ceylon cinnamon, which is better and recommended for consumption. The second is the Chinese cinnamon, which is of lower □uality, and as such is suitable for industrial production fresheners, scented candles and the like. Chinese cinnamon is not recommended in the diet because it contains more coumarin, which in larger doses can cause liver and kidney damage.

Why cinnamon is good for your health.

1. It controls blood sugar levels - Several studies have shown that cinnamon has a positive effect on blood sugar levels. Cinnamon is a popular natural remedy used by people suffering from type 2 diabetes.

2. Treating fungal Infections - Studies have shown that cinnamon oil is effective in the treatment of infections caused by Candida, such as Candida Tropicalis and Candida Albicans.

3. It relieves the symptoms caused by poisoning - Cinnamon has a strong antibacterial effect and is excellent in the treatment of stomach problems caused by salmonella and E. coli. Ground cinnamon, oil or tea of cinnamon, are effective in neutralizing stomach problems.

4. Helps in the treatment of symptoms of irritable bowel syndrome - Cinnamon drastically reduces the unpleasant symptoms of irritable bowel syndrome, especially helping with flatulence. This plant stimulates digestion and helps in the treatment of bacterial infections. In addition, cinnamon is an excellent remedy for stomach cramps.

5. Helps with osteoporosis and arthritis - Cinnamon is rich in manganese, which helps build bones, blood and connective tissues in the body. People who have less manganese in the body fre□uently suffer from osteoporosis and arthritis. Pain due to arthritis can be helped with massage oil of cinnamon or sipping tea with cinnamon.

6. Cinnamon affects cognitive development and memory - Regular consumption of cinnamon protects the health of the brain and improve concentration.

7. It is a powerful antioxidant - Cinnamon is one of the top foods rich in antioxidants. They help regenerate cells and relieve the body of harmful free radicals.

8. Helps with weight loss - Cinnamon improves circulation and can speed up metabolism.

Therefore, you will be successful in the fight with overweight.

9. Relieves muscle pain - If you feel pain in your muscles it will help to massage with cinnamon oil.

10. Lowers cholesterol and triglycerides - This spicy plant operates to prevent heart disease, to lower the level of triglycerides, cholesterol, and excess fat.

11. Cinnamon improves the health of teeth and gums - Cinnamon oil is often used in the production of chewing gum, candy freshening breath, mouthwashes, and toothpaste. This is primarily due to the strong antimicrobial effect of cinnamon.

12. Relieves colds, sore throat, and cough - Tea made from cinnamon or tea with cinnamon has a positive effect on problems caused by a cold or a sore throat, and can alleviate a cough.

13. Relieves symptoms of PMS - Since it is rich in manganese, cinnamon is a great way to reduce the unpleasant symptoms of PMS. This spice relieves spasms and relieves tension.

14. Against the symptoms of food poisoning - Cinnamon calms ailments caused by food

poisoning, can neutralize bacteria, fungi, and other microbes.

15. Regulates menstrual cycle - Cinnamon helps women who have polycystic ovaries so they can regulate the menstrual cycle.

16. Relieves a headache - If you are suffering from a migraine or regular headache, first aid can be tea of cinnamon.

Weight Loss And Cinnamon

Cinnamon, because of its aromatic spice helps give a nice taste to desserts, baked goods, coffee and oriental dishes, but the cinnamon for weight loss has been applied only recently after a series of studies conducted by scientists and experiments have confirmed its ability to reduce appetite and normalize the level of sugar in the blood. Moreover, the cinnamon was a real mine of useful substances. In the East since ancient times it is used not only in cooking but also in medicine. In conjunction with saturated fat and sugar, as is the case with cakes and pies, all the positive healing properties of cinnamon are neutralized.

According to scientific studies, cinnamon can speed sugar metabolism up to 20 times. Only a

Quarter teaspoon of cinnamon sugar promotes better digestion and reduction in blood glucose levels. This is extremely important not only for diabetics but also for effective weight loss, since the formation of fat is often associated with high blood sugar. In addition, cinnamon suppresses the appetite, which also contributes to weight loss.

Cinnamon has beneficial effects on the functioning of the gastrointestinal tract: normalize the digestive process, improves the absorption and assimilation of nutrients, and accelerates the removal of waste substances. Cinnamon has a positive effect on the kidneys. In addition, cinnamon lowers blood cholesterol levels, has antiseptic and antimicrobial action, increases vascular tone, and restores the process of blood, improves brain function and visual memory, improves mood. The use of cinnamon for weight loss allows you to get rid of extra pounds not only without harm, but also with health benefits. This spicy substance not only positively affects the operation of all systems and organs of the human body, but softly and gently cleanses the body of accumulated toxins.

You can purchase cinnamon in a store or market. It is sold in sticks or in a rock version in the form of powder. Cinnamon is also found in capsules and in tea or coffee for better ingestion. To maintain the flavor and preserve the freshness of cinnamon, it is best to store it in a tightly closed glass jar in a cool, dry place. Apply the cinnamon for effective and nearly rapid weight loss in several ways. Use Cinnamon sticks for stirring well with herbal teas, coffee, juices, yogurt and cottage cheese.

Use the combination of cinnamon with yogurt for breakfast and dinner. To prepare a drink, take a glass of 1% fat yogurt and a pinch of cinnamon. Thoroughly mix all ingredients and drink. A cup of yogurt with cinnamon can replace the dinner or breakfast, which will hold up in the morning or before dinner, without feelings of hunger.

CHAPTER THREE

Honey and Cinnamon - The Power of Two

A mixture of honey and cinnamon is a well-known remedy for many dishes. This ft is proven through studies and researches done using these two ingredients as a treatment.

The combination of the two is a wonderful and effective aid for the following diseases:

Heart Diseases

Patients who suffer from heart diseases can take honey and cinnamon in the form of breakfast spread as a substitute for jam, peanut butter and jelly.

Taking this regularly can reduce the level of cholesterol in the arteries, which in turn reduces the risk of heart attack.

The flexibility of the arteries and veins can decrease with old age, and fatty plaque may be deposited in the arteries causing them to get clogged.

In these cases, the honey-cinnamon combination may help to recover and revitalize the arteries and veins.

Arthritis

Arthritis is commonly caused by a nutrient deficiency, such as low levels of antioxidant vitamins which can have direct impact on joint function and cartilage structure. This may cause the sensitive joint tissues to be more vulnerable to the attack of free radicals. As a result, a person with nutrient deficiency may experience bone deterioration and loss of mobility.

Honey and cinnamon is found to have a major effect in relieving arthritis pain. For this purpose, the mixture of these two ingredients can be either applied externally or put into drinks.

To apply externally, mix one part honey with 2 parts of warm water. Then, add one teaspoon of cinnamon into the mixture. Apply by rubbing this mixture on the aching areas to relieve the pain.

The potential of this natural remedy to relieve arthritis has been proven in a study conducted in the Copenhagen University, Denmark. In the study, doctors gave a mixture of one tablespoon of honey and 1/2 teaspoon of cinnamon powder to 200 patients before their breakfast and within a week, 73 patients were totally relieved. Nearly all patients that were not able to walk due to arthritis could start walking painlessly within a month of treatment and did not show any symptoms of arthritis.

Hair Loss

Combining cinnamon and honey with olive oil can stimulate the hair growth. This mixture has been a very popular folk medicine and used by those who suffer from hair loss or baldness.

Warm olive oil, 1 tablespoon of honey and 1 teaspoon of cinnamon powder can be mixed together to form a soft paste. This paste is then applied onto the scalp and left for approximately 30 minutes before shampooing. This mixture has been a very popular folk medicine.

Stomach upsetness

The combination of honey and cinnamon powder helps to settle an upset stomach which is due to infection or indigestion. It also works as an aid for gastritis and stomach ulcers.

Cold

Drinking hot water with honey and cinnamon can provide a □uick relief for common and severe cold. Put 1 tablespoon of lukewarm honey and 1/4 spoon of cinnamon powder into the water and drink a cup every 2-3 hours. It helps prevent mucus buildup and encourage you to sweat. Cinnamon oil mixed with honey is an effective remedy for colds.

Shock and fatigue

Another traditional remedy that used to be practiced in the earlier times was combining honey and cinnamon to treat shock and anxiety. Add a pinch of cinnamon to a cup of hot water, add half a teaspoon of honey and freshly s□ueezed juice from two or three lemons. This mixture is believed to be anti-spasmodic and has a calming, relaxing effect on the body.

For those of you who suffer from common fatigue, now there's a great and effective way to boost energy using honey and cinnamon. A contemporary research on this matter was conducted by Dr. Milton Abbozza and he recommended taking a glass of water with 1/2 tablespoon of honey, and sprinkled with cinnamon powder. This should be taken daily in the morning and in the afternoon. Within a week, one can notice the increase in body stamina.

CHAPTER FOUR

CINNAMON OIL

Cinnamon Oil is derived from a tree that is recognized by two botanical names – Cinnamomum zeylanicum and Cinnamomum vervun – both of which refer to the same tree. This is the species considered to be true Cinnamon. The English name for this spice is rooted in the term "amomon," or "qinnamon," the Arabic and Hebraic word for "fragrant spice plant." Harvested and processed as both a spice and an essential oil, it is cultivated and exported globally. Cinnamon was also given the Early Modern English names of "canel" and "canella," which were rooted in the Latin word for "tube," due to the inner bark's tendency to naturally form a tube shape as it dries and retracts into itself. Cinnamon Essential Oil may be obtained from either the tree's outer bark or its leaves, hence the two main varieties are Cinnamon Bark Essential Oil and Cinnamon Leaf Essential Oil.

BENEFITS OF CINNAMON OIL

The main chemical constituents of Cinnamon Bark Essential Oil and Cinnamon Leaf Essential Oils, albeit in varying amounts, are Cinnamaldehyde, Cinnamyl Acetate, Eugenol, and Eugenol Acetate.

Used in aromatherapy applications, Cinnamon Essential Oil is known to help diminish the feelings of depression, faintness, and exhaustion. It is reputed to relax the body enough to stimulate the libido, making it an effective natural aphrodisiac. Its anti-rheumatic ualities address joint and muscle pain, and it is known to be advantageous for strengthening immunity and thereby reducing the symptoms of colds and the flu. Its ability to enhance circulation helps reduce the pain associated with headaches and makes it beneficial for enhancing the function of the digestive system. When diffused throughout the home or other indoor environments, its scent freshens and deodorizes while emitting its characteristic warm, uplifting, and relaxing fragrance that is known to have a therapeutic grounding and soothing effect. Furthermore, Cinnamon is known to have calming and tonic effects on the mind that are reputed to result in an improved cognitive function. Its ability to reduce nervous tension helps advance information retention, extends the attention span, enhances the memory and reduces the risk of memory loss.

Used cosmetically or topically in general, Cinnamon Essential Oil is reputed to calm dry skin and to effectively alleviate aches, pains, and stiffness experienced in the muscles and joints and in the digestive system. Its antibacterial properties make it ideal for use in addressing acne, rashes, and infections. Its anti-oxidant properties help to slow the look of aging.

Used medicinally, Cinnamon Essential Oil is reputed to effectively reduce inflammation, eliminate viruses, and boost immunity. Its ability to enhance circulation facilitates pain relief while improving the function of the metabolism. When applied to cuts, it is known to exhibit coagulant properties that help stem the flow of blood from cuts, thereby assisting the healing process. Cinnamon Oil is known to benefit the respiratory system by reducing the symptoms of colds and the flu, such as a sore throat, nasal congestion, and headaches. Its carminative properties make it ideal for use in alleviating digestive discomforts such as gas.

HOW IS CINNAMON OIL EXTRACTED?

Cinnamon Leaf Oil and Cinnamon Bark Oil are both derived from the steam distillation of each of these respective parts. Before extracting the oil from the bark, Cinnamon sticks are mashed or broken into small pieces and placed inside the distillation flask, which is connected to the steam generator and to a condenser, where oil condenses. From there, it passes through a separator where it is collected.

Although they share similarities, their benefits are diverse and they are thus best suited to different applications. The extract from the bark is reputed to have a robust and perfume-like aroma that is reminiscent of ground Cinnamon's aroma. Its color generally ranges from a clear yellow to a deep reddish-brown that is characteristic of the spice itself. This variety is believed to be the more potent of the two. Conversely, the extract from the leaves is known to have an aroma that is spicy and musky. It is generally lighter in color and often appears to be a brownish-yellow.

CINNAMON OIL USES

The uses for Cinnamon Essential Oil are abundant, ranging from medicinal and odorous to cosmetic. Its many forms include massage oils and gels, face creams, lotions, soaps, shampoos, hair oils, room sprays, perfumes, and candles.

Used in aromatherapy applications, Cinnamon's scent can be diffused to address lethargy, irritability, unhealthy cravings, and a tendency to overindulge when eating, as it is reputed to facilitate the sensation of being full. Furthermore, it is known to relieve symptoms of colds, severe coughs, and sneezing. For an invigorating Cinnamon Oil blend that boosts immunity, eases congestion, and relieves stress, diffuse a blend of 1 drop Cinnamon Essential Oil (Bark or Leaf), 1 drop Rosemary Essential Oil, 1 drop Eucalyptus Essential Oil, 1 drop Clove Essential Oil, and 1 drop Orange Essential Oil. Alternatively, Cinnamon Oil may be combined with Tea Tree or Lemon essential oils for a blend that boosts the mood and energy levels.

Used in cosmetic applications, Cinnamon Oil is known to effectively soothe dry skin. For a Cinnamon formulation that functions as a therapeutic and rejuvenating moisturizer, mix 1 drop of Cinnamon Oil into a regular face cream and massage a small amount of the mixture into the skin at night before bedtime. If the cream is not fast-absorbing, continue massaging it into the skin until it is completely absorbed. Excess cream can be wiped off with a cotton pad. This regimen can be continued nightly to diminish the appearance of aging.

For a Cinnamon shampoo that is reputed to stimulate hair growth and to address dandruff, thinning hair, and hair fall, combine 5-6 drops of Cinnamon Essential Oil with 5 Tbsp. Olive Carrier Oil and massage this blend into the scalp. Allow it to soak in for 45 minutes before washing it out with a natural shampoo. This shampoo regimen may be repeated up to 3 times a week to cleanse hair and stimulate healthier and stronger growth. Alternatively, a drop of Cinnamon Oil may be added to a regular shampoo to maintain hair health, add luster to dull strands, and to work as a preventative measure against head lice.

Cinnamon Oil is a beneficial ingredient for a natural face wash intended to enhance skin health by reducing inflammation, redness, and swelling while also eliminating harmful bacteria, preventing acne, and soothing infections. In a bowl, simply combine 1 Tbsp. Organic Coconut Carrier Oil, 3 Tbsp. Raw Honey, 1 Tbsp. Apple Cider Vinegar, 20 drops Cinnamon Essential Oil, and 2 capsules of live probiotics. With a hand blender, mix all the ingredients together thoroughly, then pour the mixture into a convenient bottle or dispenser. Store this Honey and Cinnamon Oil Facial Cleanser in a cool place when it is not being used. Apply this cleanser to the face in the method of a usual face wash.

Used in medicinal applications, Cinnamon Oil's warming properties make it ideal for soothing skin and muscles that are sore and tender. It can be included in an anti-septic massage blend to address arthritis, bronchitis, diarrhea, chills, flu, cold, indigestion, spasms, nausea, and infection. For a pain-relieving massage blend, dilute 3 drops of Cinnamon Essential Oil in 2 Tbsp. of a Carrier Oil such as Olive and massage it into the affected area. Regularly applying this massage blend is known to soothe inflammation, stiffness, muscle knots, and back pain. Massaging this oil blend into the abdomen for 5 minutes can help tone the digestive system, facilitate the release of excess gas, and ease bloating.

For a massage blend that combines other beneficial oils that relieve sore joints, combine 6 drops of Cinnamon Essential Oil, 4 drops of Clove Bud Essential Oil, 3 drops of Rosemary Essential Oil, 3 drops of Cedarwood Essential Oil, 2 drops of Neroli Essential Oil, 1 drop of Ylang-Ylang Essential Oil, 1 drop of Thyme Essential Oil, 60 ml (2 oz.) of a Carrier Oil of personal preference. This blend can be massaged into the affected areas daily until the pain subsides.

Cinnamon Oil can be diluted and used for an aromatic bath with a sweet and spicy scent. For a Cinnamon Bath Salt Soak, combine 3 ½ cups Epsom salts, 1-2 Tbsp. ground Cinnamon, and 5-10 drops Cinnamon Essential Oil in a large bowl, then thoroughly mix all the ingredients. Store the blend in an air-tight container until it is time to use it. In the bathtub, toss a handful of the salts under running tap water to ensure that the salts are properly dispersed. Ensure that they dissolve completely in the water before entering the tub. Alternatively, a bath salt blend can be made with 2 cups of salts, 1 cup of Baking Soda, 10 drops of Cinnamon Essential Oil, 5 drops of Eucalyptus Essential Oil, 5 drops Rosemary Essential Oil, 5 drops Lavender Essential Oil, 5 drops Peppermint Essential Oil, and 1 Tbsp. Carrier Oil.

CHAPTER FIVE

CINNAMON STICKS

What is so darned appealing about whole cinnamon sticks? We're not talking about the red-hot, brown colored powder you find littering coffee condiment counters, or the mysterious throat-burning flavor that haunts candies, drinks, and ready-to-eat pastries. No, this is an investigation of the true spice, the classic spice, the flaky, copper □uills that have fueled global culinary desire for thousands of years. There's a reason, or rather many reasons, the cinnamon stick keeps popping up: etched in Greek amphora, featured in Renaissance paintings, and adorning every pastry on Instagram.

The case for whole cinnamon sticks is not a hard one to make. First is the obvious advantage to keeping spices whole: increasing shelf life. Cinnamon sticks can be used differently than ground cinnamon, but can still be ground if you just need a pinch. Beyond the practicalities, a true cinnamon stick is a historical lesson, study in craftsmanship, and sensory delight all rolled into one. Ground or not, it's a spice that's bound to stick around.

CEYLON CINNAMON

Before we talk about cinnamon, we should first discuss the sticky subject of "cinnamon." The word cinnamon is used to describe two different spices: true cinnamon, or Ceylon cinnamon, and cassia, or Vietnamese cinnamon (also called Chinese cinnamon). The technical details are here, but suffice it to say that cassia is a larger and less delicate spice. A few legal loopholes allow the cheaper cassia cinnamon to be sold as true, or Ceylon, cinnamon. You can differentiate the two in a number of ways.

Cassia

Cassia is a visusally very different creature, with a single thick layer of bark curling in on itself. Cassia trees contain a lot of flavor at full maturity, and can actually improve with age. A 30-year-old cassia tree packs a powerful, long-lasting bite. Cinnamon trees, on the other hand, are harvested very early when their shoots are still supple and young, with concentrated flavor. From the outset, you're starting with a much thinner bark.

Cinnamon Bark

The process of turning a cinnamon tree shoot into a cinnamon stick (technically, a cinnamon stick is called a quill) is highly specialized task. Shoots are first harvested, then the outer bark is removed. Artisans then scrape the length of the shoots to make the inner bark pliable and encourage oil to come to the surface. After being soaked in water, the cinnamon shoots are split down the middle and left in climate controlled rooms to allow the inner bark to separate from the wood.

After a few hours or days, the soon-to-be sticks are rolled onto thin, 42-inch long metal canes and hung to dry for several days. Finally, the finished quills are stored under lock and key: their great value and light weight makes them prime targets for thieves (yeah, cinnamon rustlers are a thing).

CINNAMON ROLL

The rolling process itself has a profound impact on the quality of the cinnamon and deserves its own section with a pun and everything (I am on a roll after all). Higher grade quills require thin, uniform layers, which can only come from a single, long layer of bark. Any knots or defects in the tree, as well as error by the craftsperson, translate to a short piece of bark, which will in turn become a wide, warped, and lower □uality cinnamon stick.

Cinnamon Peeler

So, as you might imagine, the role of roller is an exclusive one in Sri Lanka. The services of cinnamon harvesters, peelers, and rollers are so in demand that few (if any) plantations are able to keep any on staff. Most cinnamon today is processed by a roving guild of hereditary artisans, who arrive at the end of the rainy season and work for days or weeks straight until they've dried as much cinnamon as possible.

What happens with cinnamon shoots that don't become cinnamon sticks? You may recall that true cinnamon comes from recently grown shoots, so it is possible that an unharvested tree may not yield any cinnamon for years to come. The crop is simply lost.

Hidden inside every tiny □uill lies this unspeakable craft. From the first harvest to the exhaustive peeling to the precise rolling, a chain of meticulous care transforms an everyday tree into one of the most sought after commodities in history. Behind all this is the threat of error: slice it wrong, roll it too loosely, work too slowly, or come too late in the season and all that effort might as well be compost. It is compost.

CHAPTER SIX

Cinnamon Powder

Cinnamon is the bark of the tropical trees. It is brown in colour and has a sweet taste that finishes off with a sharp, pungent flavor. This bark is ground to prepare Cinnamon powder, which has a coarse texture. The cinnamon powder comes in the form of a sprinkler can or in packet form.

Is Cinnamon Powder Good For Health?

Cinnamon powder is packed with health benefits to your body. This powder is rich in Calcium, Magnesium and other important nutrients. Besides, Cinnamon powder also offers anti-bacterial and anti-viral properties to ward off infection-causing microbes, along with boosting your immune system. It also contains many Cancer-fighting agents to shield your body against deadly diseases.

Uses of cinnamon powder

1. Regulates Blood Sugar:

As per research, Cinnamon powder is highly efficient in lowering your blood sugar levels. If taken in limited amounts, cinnamon powder can really be helpful in ensuring control over spiked up blood sugar levels by almost 24%. This makes it a perfect choice for diabetic patients. Along with your regular medication, taking a pinch of Cinnamon powder per day can help do wonders!

2. Helps Control Bad Cholesterol:

Cinnamon powder is also effective in lowering the cholesterol levels, that can block your arteries. This is one of the best advantages of Cinnamon powder! To decrease the levels of LDL also known as bad cholesterol in the body, cinnamon powder can work really well. This helps in keeping away cardiovascular problems and diseases. However, make sure that you do not exceed the limit of 6 grams per day of cinnamon powder.

3. Reduces Arthritis Pain:

Another of the very good and effective benefits of cinnamon comes in the form of pain reduction in case of joint inflammation also known as arthritis. The anti-inflammatory agents in Cinnamon powder can treat painful conditions like Gout and other tissue disorders. It also contains certain antioxidants like Cinnamaldehyde and Cinnamic acid which can reduce the cell damage.

4. Reduces PMS problems:

Have you ever tried a cup of fresh cinnamon tea made from cinnamon powder during your periods? If not, then try it this time around and see how well it helps you in treatment of the cramps and abdomen pain that tags along. Cinnamon powder can also regulate your periods as well as heavy bleeding disorders. This is one of the major Dalchini powder health benefits!

5. Treats Infertility:

If you are facing problems in your sex life or having issues with conceiving, Cinnamon can come to your aid. There are some natural chemicals in cinnamon powder known as cinnamaldehyde. this is known to help improve the levels of progesterone and decreases testosterone in women and balances the levels of fertility. A balance in hormone is always good for fertile levels as well as sexual health.

CONCLUSION

The information contained in this book is not designed to treat, cure, diagnose, or replace the advice given by health care professionals. Information was gained from research on the benefits of adding cinnamon to a lifestyle routine. To be used as a supplemental informative guide only, and should be used by you in any manner that you see fit

. Previous study also shows ground cinnamon to be effective in killing bacteria that cause bad breath as demonstrated in an experiment where cinnamon-flavored gum was used. Cinnamon is also believed to have anti-coagulating properties. The cinnamaldehyde content in cinnamon is responsible for the thinning of the blood but it also prevents unnecessary clotting of the blood platelets.

Cinnamon powder is an extremely rich source of calcium and manganese necessary for strengthening our bones, iron for the proper transport of oxygen in the blood and dietary fiber.

Daily doses of ground cinnamon mixed with your coffee or tea, your favorite dessert, your favorite recipes with cinnamon, or simply sniffing its scent will have intangible but invaluable benefits of cinnamon to your body. You don't have to worry about buying cinnamon powder because it is available in your favorite supermarket, in health food stores, and drug stores near your area. It is also available online with the appropriate cinnamon nutrition facts you need to know.